F
SCOTTISH
TEATIME
RECIPES

compiled by
Johanna Mathie

Index

Front Cover: Neist Point Lighthouse, Back Cover: Whisky Barrels

Printed & published by Dorrigo, Manchester, England © Copyright

Pitcaithly Bannock

8 oz. flour   **2 oz. caster sugar**
4 oz. butter   **1 oz. chopped almonds**
1 oz. mixed candied peel

Set oven to 325°F or Mark 3. Well grease and flour a baking sheet. Cream the butter and sugar together in a bowl until very soft. Add the flour, with the almonds and peel, and rub in very well. It is essential to continue working the mixture until the warmth of the hands has sufficiently amalgamated the butter and flour to produce a soft dough. Form the dough, on the baking sheet, into a round about 5 inches in diameter and 1½ to 1¾ inches thick, moulding with warm hands to consolidate. Prick all over with a fork. Bake for 40 to 60 minutes until light brown. Leave for about 10 minutes then transfer to a wire rack. When cold, cut carefully with a sharp knife into slices about ½ to ⅝ inch thick and serve lightly buttered.

Petticoat Tails

| 8 oz. flour | 4 oz. butter |
| 4 oz. cornflour or rice flour | 4 oz. icing sugar |

Caster sugar for dredging

Set the oven to 350°F or Mark 4. Grease a baking sheet. Cream the butter and icing sugar together in a bowl. Sift in the flours and work into a smooth dough; if the dough is too dry a little water can be added to moisten. Divide into two. Roll out on a floured surface and shape into two thin rounds. Place on the sheet and prick all over with a fork. Mark each round into six triangles. Bake for about 20-25 minutes until pale golden in colour. Sprinkle with caster sugar while still warm. Cut into the triangles and cool on a wire rack.

Fairy Pools, Isle of Skye

Apple Gingerbread

½ lb. cooking apples   3 oz. butter
Sugar to taste   6 oz. self-raising flour
3 oz. demerara sugar   1 teaspoon ground ginger
¼ lb. golden syrup   ¼ teaspoon ground cloves
1 egg

Set oven to 350°F or Mark 4. Grease an 8 inch x 6 inch baking tin. Peel, core and slice the apples. Put into a pan with a little water and sufficient sugar to taste. Stew gently until tender, then mash and cool. In a separate pan melt the syrup and butter and demerara sugar together gently until dissolved. Leave to cool. Sift the flour, ginger, and cloves into a bowl and make a well in centre. Add the egg to the syrup mixture and beat well into the flour. Stir in the mashed apples and continue to beat all well together. Turn into the tin and cook for 30 minutes until firm. Leave to stand for a few minutes in the tin before turning out to cool on a wire rack; cut into slices.

Potato Scones

½ lb. cooked potatoes   ½ oz. butter
2 oz. flour   Pinch of salt
A little milk or buttermilk to bind

To test for the correct heat of the girdle sprinkle it with a little flour.
If the flour browns at once it is too hot; it should take a few seconds to turn colour.

Grease a girdle or heavy frying-pan. Mash the potatoes with the butter and a little milk. Mix with a spoon. Add the salt and a little of the flour. Use the fingers to knead the mixture, adding more flour until it is all taken up and the dough is fairly stiff. Turn out on to a floured surface. Roll out to ¼ inch thick and cut into rounds using a breakfast cup as a cutter. Place on the hot greased girdle or frying-pan. Cook for about 2 minutes until the underside is brown. Turn and repeat on the other side. Serve piping hot, spread with butter.

Dundee Cake

8 oz. flour	4 oz. sultanas
6 oz. caster sugar	2 oz. candied peel
6 oz. butter or margarine	1 oz. ground almonds
4 eggs	1 teaspoon mixed spice
4 oz. currants	1 teaspoon baking powder
4 oz. raisins	½ teaspoon salt

1 oz. split, blanched almonds

Set oven to 325°F or Mark 3. Grease an 8 inch round cake tin and line with greaseproof paper. Cream the fat and sugar in a bowl. Sift the flour, salt and spice together. Add the eggs and the flour mixture alternately to the creamed fat, beating them in well. Add the baking powder to the last of the flour. Stir in the ground almonds. Add the fruit and peel. Gently mix. Put into the tin. Arrange the split almonds evenly on the top of the cake. Bake for about 2 hours. After the first hour, if the top is browning too quickly, cover with greaseproof paper. Allow the cake to cool slightly in the tin before turning on to a wire rack. The cake will keep for several weeks if wrapped in kitchen foil.

Eilean Donan Castle

Oatcakes

8 oz. fine (pinhead) oatmeal   ½ teaspoon bicarbonate of soda
Pinch of salt   2 tablespoons dripping or melted butter (bacon fat is ideal)
¼ pint hot water   A little extra oatmeal for the rolling

To test for the correct heat of the girdle sprinkle it with a little flour. If the flour browns
at once it is too hot; it should take a few seconds to turn colour.

Set oven to 375°F or Mark 5 or heat a girdle or a heavy frying-pan. Mix the oatmeal, the bicarbonate of soda and salt together in a bowl. Add the melted fat and the hot water. Stir well until it makes a soft paste. Sprinkle some oatmeal on a board. Form the dough into a round and roll it out as thinly as possible, adding oatmeal to the surface as necessary, to prevent sticking. Brush off the excess oatmeal. Cut the dough into 4 or 6 pieces. To oven bake: place on a large ungreased baking sheet. Bake for 15-20 minutes. To girdle bake: bake on a hot girdle or frying-pan until the edges begin to curl. Turn over and cook the other side. Do not let the oatcakes brown; they should be a pale fawn colour. Put on a wire rack to cool. They are delicious served with cheese.

Buttermilk Bread

1 lb. flour	1 teaspoon sugar
1 teaspoon cream of tartar	1 oz. butter
1 teaspoon baking soda	2 breakfast cups of buttermilk
1 teaspoon salt	or thick soured milk

Set oven to 425°F or Mark 7. Grease and flour a baking sheet. Mix all the dry ingredients together in a bowl. Lightly rub in the butter. Add the buttermilk and mix into a light, soft dough. Divide into two and shape into rounds on a lightly floured surface. Place the rounds on the baking sheet and bake for about 20 minutes. Serve sliced with butter.

Honey and Whisky Cake

**6 oz. self-raising flour   6 oz. butter   6 oz. soft brown sugar   3 eggs, beaten
4 tablespoons whisky   Grated rind of a small orange**

**Butter icing:
6 oz. icing sugar   2 oz. butter
2 tablespoons clear honey
Juice from the small orange
Toasted flaked almonds to decorate**

Set oven to 375°F or Mark 5. Grease two 7 inch sandwich tins. Cream the butter and sugar together in a bowl. Add the orange rind. Beat in the eggs one at a time and whisk until the mixture is pale and fluffy. Sift in about half the flour and add the whisky. Fold into the mixture. Sift in the remaining flour and fold in. Divide the mixture equally between the two tins and smooth the tops. Bake for 20-25 minutes until light golden. Turn out on to a wire rack to cool. To make the icing, put the butter into a mixing bowl. Add the honey and one tablespoon of the orange juice. Sift in the icing sugar slowly and work the mixture gradually until the ingredients are combined. Sandwich the cakes together with half of the buttercream. Smooth the remainder over the top of the cake and decorate with toasted almonds.

Glenfinnan Railway Viaduct

Old-fashioned Raspberry Buns

8 oz. self-raising flour	1 egg, beaten
3 oz. caster sugar	⅔ dessertspoon milk
4 oz. margarine	Raspberry jam

Caster sugar to dust

Set oven to 425°F or Mark 7. Grease and flour baking sheets. Sift the flour into a bowl and rub in the margarine. Add the sugar and the beaten egg with enough milk to make a fairly stiff consistency. Divide the mixture into about walnut-size balls and place on baking sheets, allowing space for them to spread slightly during cooking. Make a small hole in the centre of each ball and spoon in a little raspberry jam. Pinch the edges together again. Dust lightly with caster sugar. Bake for 10 minutes then reduce heat to 350°F or Mark 4 and bake for a further 5 minutes. The buns should be light golden in colour. Cool on a wire rack.

Border Tart

8 oz. shortcrust pastry	1 egg, beaten
2 oz. butter	5 oz. mixed dried fruit
2 oz. dark soft brown sugar	1 oz. walnuts, chopped

1 oz. glacé cherries, chopped

FOR DECORATION
4 oz. icing sugar
1 tablespoon water

Set oven to 375°F or Mark 5. Grease a 7 inch round flan tin. Gently melt the butter and sugar together in a pan. Remove from the heat and leave to cool. Meanwhile roll out the pastry on a floured surface and line the flan tin. Add the beaten egg to the butter/sugar mixture and mix well. Then add the mixed dried fruit, chopped nuts and chopped glacé cherries and beat well. Put the mixture in to the tin, level the top and bake for 20-25 minutes. Allow to cool. Mix together the icing sugar and the water and use to drizzle a lattice pattern over the tart. Turn out when quite cold.

Scotch Pancakes

4 oz. self-raising flour   **1 oz. caster sugar**
Small pinch salt   **1 egg**
¼ pint milk

Grease a girdle or heavy frying-pan. Whisk the egg with the milk. Sift the flour and salt into a bowl. Add the sugar. Pour in the egg and milk mixture. Mix with a wooden spoon until the batter is smooth. Alternatively put all the ingredients in a food processor and blend until smooth. Heat the greased girdle or frying-pan; test the temperature by dropping a small spoonful of batter on the girdle and if the underside turns brown in under a minute the heat is sufficient. Drop tablespoonsful of batter on to the girdle. When the surface is covered in bubbles turn with a slice and cook for half a minute on the other side. Wrap the cooked pancakes in a clean tea towel to keep moist. They are excellent spread with butter and jam.

Buchanness Lighthouse

Treacle Scones

8 oz. self-raising flour	2 tablespoons black treacle
2 oz. butter	or golden syrup
1 oz. caster sugar	Pinch of salt
½ teaspoon ground cinnamon	Milk to mix, approx ¼ pint

Set oven to 425°F or Mark 7. Grease a baking sheet. Sift the flour and salt into a bowl and rub in the butter. Mix in the sugar and cinnamon. Add the treacle or syrup and sufficient milk to make a soft dough. Turn on to a floured surface and knead gently. The dough should be fairly moist and elastic. Roll out to about ½ inch thick. Cut into rounds with a 2½ inch pastry cutter. Place on the baking sheet, brush with a little milk and bake for 10-15 minutes until golden in colour. Cool on a wire rack. Serve split in half and buttered.

Abernethy Biscuits

8 oz. flour   **½ teaspoon baking powder**   **3 oz. butter**   **3 oz. caster sugar**
½ teaspoon caraway seeds (optional)   **1 egg, beaten**   **1 tablespoon milk**

Set oven to 350°F or Mark 4. Grease a baking sheet. Sift the flour and baking powder into a bowl. Rub in the butter well until the mixture resembles breadcrumbs. Add the sugar and the caraway seeds (if required). Add the beaten egg and the milk and mix thoroughly until it forms a sticky dough. Turn the dough on to a floured surface and roll out thinly. Cut into rounds with a 2 inch biscuit cutter. Place on the baking sheet and cook for about 10-15 minutes until pale golden in colour.

Bells Bridge

Light Plum Cake

8 oz. flour	2 oz. currants
4 oz. brown sugar	2 oz. raisins
4 oz. butter or margarine	2 oz. mixed peel
2 eggs, beaten	1 teaspoon bicarbonate of soda
2–3 tablespoons milk	2 teaspoons mixed spice

Set oven to 375°F or Mark 5. Grease a 7 inch round cake tin and line with greaseproof paper. Cream the fat and sugar together in a bowl. Sift together the flour, mixed spice and bicarbonate of soda and add, alternately with the beaten eggs and the milk, to the creamed mixture. The mixture should be quite moist. Mix in the fruits. Transfer to the tin and bake for 1¼ hours, reducing the heat to 350°F or Mark 4 after 30 minutes. If the top starts to brown cover with foil. When cooked turn out on to a wire rack and allow to cool.

Marmalade and Ginger Slice

8 oz. flour	8 oz. orange marmalade
8 oz. golden syrup	1 teaspoon baking powder
4 oz. butter	1 teaspoon ground ginger
	1 egg, beaten

Set oven to 350°F or Mark 4. Grease an 8 inch square cake tin. Melt the syrup and butter in a pan over a very gentle heat. Stir in the marmalade. Leave to cool. Sift the dry ingredients into a bowl. Make a well in the centre and pour in the syrup mixture and the beaten egg. Beat well until thoroughly blended. Turn into the tin and cook for about 45 minutes until firm and golden in colour. Cool on a wire rack and cut into slices.

Ayrshire Shortbread

4 oz. ground rice	4 oz. caster sugar
4 oz. flour	1 egg yolk, beaten
4 oz. butter	1 tablespoon double cream
1 drop vanilla essence	

Set oven to 350°F or Mark 4. Grease a baking sheet. Sift the flour and ground rice into a bowl. Rub in the butter and add the caster sugar. Add the beaten egg yolk, the cream and the vanilla essence to bind the mixture. Knead well on a floured surface to a stiff consistency. Do not add any extra moisture. Roll out thinly. Prick with a fork and cut into fingers. Place the fingers on the baking sheet and bake for about 15-20 minutes until golden brown in colour.

Girdle Scones

8 oz. flour	**1 oz. butter**
½ teaspoon bicarbonate of soda	**1 teaspoon golden syrup**
½ teaspoon cream of tartar	**8 fl. oz. buttermilk,**
½ teaspoon baking powder	**full cream milk or sour milk**

To test for the correct heat of the girdle sprinkle it with a little flour.
If the flour browns at once it is too hot; it should take a few seconds to turn colour.

Sift the flour into a bowl. Add the other dry ingredients and mix. Rub in the butter. Add the syrup and the milk and mix with a palette knife to a soft consistency. Turn on to a floured surface and roll quickly and lightly (handle as little as possible) to about ¾ inch thick. Cut into rounds. Grease and heat the girdle or heavy frying-pan (it should be quite hot). Lift the scones on to the girdle and, with a slice or broad knife, turn once until brown on both sides. Serve freshly baked, spread with butter.

Stag in the Highlands

Whisky and Apple Jelly

6 lb. cooking apples   **Water**
Granulated sugar   **Whisky**

Wash the apples, cut away any bad bits and quarter them. Place in a large preserving pan and just cover with water. Boil until quite soft but not pulpy. Put into a jelly bag and allow to drip overnight. Do not try to hurry the dripping process or the jelly will be cloudy. Measure the juice and allow one pound of sugar to each pint of liquid. Put the juice and sugar into the pan and stir over a moderate heat until the sugar dissolves. Bring to the boil, stirring continuously, skimming off the scum from time to time. To test if the jelly will set drop a little on to a cold plate. When setting point is reached, remove from the heat and allow to rest for a few minutes. Add about a tablespoonful of whisky to the juice (quantity according to taste). Pour immediately into warm jars and seal. Do not use for at least 3 months.

Selkirk Bannock

8 oz. flour	**¼ pt warm milk**
½ teaspoon salt	**½ oz. fresh yeast**
1½ oz. butter	**8 oz. sultanas**
1½ oz. granulated sugar	**Beaten egg to glaze**

Butter a 1 lb. loaf tin. Dissolve the sugar in the milk and stir in the yeast until thoroughly mixed. Leave in a warm place for 15 minutes. Meanwhile sift the flour and salt into a bowl. Add the butter and rub in. Make a well in the centre and pour in the yeast mixture. Mix together vigorously until it forms a soft dough. Turn on to a floured surface. Knead gently and shape into a ball. Transfer to a greased bowl, cover and leave to rise in a warm place for 30 minutes. Then work in the sultanas with the hands so they are evenly distributed. Re-form the dough ball and leave to rise for 30 minutes. Finally transfer to the tin; leave to rise for 45 minutes. Brush with beaten egg. Bake for 20 minutes in a pre-heated oven at 350°F or Mark 4 until golden in colour. Turn on to a wire rack to cool. Serve sliced thinly and buttered.

Paradise Cake

8 oz. shortcrust pastry	2 tablespoons chopped glacé cherries
Raspberry jam	2 tablespoons chopped walnuts
4 oz. margarine	2 tablespoons ground almonds
4 oz. caster sugar	Vanilla essence
1 egg, beaten	Caster sugar for dusting

Set oven to 350°F or Mark 4. Grease an 11 inch x 7 inch baking tin. Roll out the pastry on a floured surface and use to line the tin. Bake blind for 10 minutes. Meanwhile cream the margarine and caster sugar together in a bowl. Stir in the beaten egg and the cherries, walnuts and almonds. Add the vanilla essence and mix well. Spread a layer of raspberry jam over the bottom of the pastry case. Spoon the mixture on to the jam, level off and bake for 30-35 minutes. Sprinkle with caster sugar and leave to cool in the tin. When cold cut into squares.

Flapjacks

8 oz. rolled oats   **3 oz. caster sugar**
4 oz. butter or margarine **2 tablespoons golden syrup**

Set oven to 350°F or Mark 4. Grease an 11 inch x 7 inch baking tin. Gently heat the butter or margarine, sugar and golden syrup together in a pan until all are melted. Gradually stir in the rolled oats, combining well with the syrup mixture. Press into the tin and cook for about 20 minutes. Mark into fingers and leave in the tin to cool. When cold turn out and break up; the flapjacks should still be soft and moist.

Light Family Fruit Square

8 oz. self-raising flour	Pinch of salt
6 oz. butter or margarine	2 tablespoons milk
6 oz. caster sugar	3 oz. mixed dried fruit
3 eggs	Grated zest of one orange

Set oven to 350°F or Mark 4. Line an 8 inch square cake tin with buttered greaseproof paper. Cream together the butter or margarine and sugar in a bowl. Add the eggs one at a time, beating each well into the mixture. Sift the flour and salt and fold in gradually with the milk. Add the fruit and the orange zest, ensuring it is evenly mixed in. Spoon the mixture into the tin and bake for 40-45 minutes until a skewer inserted into the cake comes out clean. Turn on to a wire rack to cool and then cut into squares.

Butterscotch Biscuits

12 oz. self-raising flour   **1 egg, beaten**
4 oz. margarine   **8 oz. brown sugar**
½ teaspoon salt   **1 teaspoon vanilla essence**

Set oven to 350°F or Mark 4. Grease a baking sheet. Melt the sugar, margarine and vanilla essence together in a saucepan very gently over a low heat. Remove from the heat. When the mixture has cooled add the beaten egg and mix together. Sift the flour and salt into a bowl. Make a well in the centre and pour in the cooled egg/fat/sugar mixture. Knead into a stiff dough. This will be fairly dry, but it needs no extra moisture. Roll out the dough on a floured surface into ½ inch thickness and cut out the biscuits with a 2 inch biscuit cutter. Place on the baking sheet with sufficient space to allow them to spread. Bake for 20 minutes until light golden in colour.

Falkirk Wheel

Brandy Wafers

2 oz. golden syrup	**2 oz. caster sugar**
2 oz. butter	**½ teaspoon brandy**
2 oz. flour	**½ teaspoon ground ginger**

Set oven to 450°F or Mark 8. Grease baking sheets. Melt the butter, syrup and sugar together in a saucepan over a very gentle heat. Stir in the flour, ground ginger and the brandy. Beat together for about 5 minutes. Drop small teaspoonsful on to the baking sheet, spaced well apart. Bake for 5 minutes until pale golden brown in colour. Roll immediately, while still hot, around the greased handle of a large wooden spoon. Set aside to cool. These are delicious filled with freshly whipped cream.

Tantallon Biscuits

4 oz. butter
4 oz. caster sugar
4 oz. flour
4 oz. cornflour or rice flour

Pinch of bicarbonate of soda
Level teaspoon grated lemon rind
2 medium eggs, beaten
Icing sugar for dusting

Set oven to 375°F or Mark 5. Grease a baking sheet. Cream the butter and sugar together in a bowl until light and fluffy. Add the sifted flours, bicarbonate of soda and lemon rind and combine together. Mix in beaten egg in small amounts, combining well with each addition, sufficient just to produce a soft but not sticky dough. Turn out the dough on to a floured surface and knead quickly and gently, but do not over-handle. Roll out thinly and cut into rounds with a 2½ inch pastry cutter. Arrange on the baking sheet and bake for 20 to 25 minutes until light golden in colour. Transfer to a wire rack to cool and dust with icing sugar.

Oatmeal Gingerbread

6 oz. flour	1 teaspoon ground ginger
2 oz. oatmeal	1 teaspoon mixed spice
2 oz. soft brown sugar	1 large egg, beaten
2 oz. butter	1 level teaspoon bicarbonate of soda
2 tablespoons black treacle	3 tablespoons milk

Set oven to 350°F or Mark 4. Line a 7 inch square baking tin with buttered greaseproof paper. Put the butter, sugar and treacle together in a saucepan and heat gently until the fat melts. Sieve the flour and bicarbonate of soda into a bowl and add the oatmeal and spices. Add the melted treacle mixture, the beaten egg and the milk. Stir well until blended. Pour into the tin and bake for about 45 minutes. Cool in the tin for about 10 minutes then turn out on to a wire rack.

Scone Palace

Scottish Brown Bread

6 oz. wholemeal flour	¼ pint milk
4 oz. white flour	1 teaspoon bicarbonate of soda
1 tablespoon golden syrup	1 teaspoon cream of tartar

Pinch of salt

Set oven to 325°F or Mark 3. Grease a 1 lb. loaf tin. Mix the flours, salt, bicarbonate of soda and cream of tartar together in a bowl. Add the golden syrup and mix with sufficient of the milk to form a soft dough. Turn out on to a floured surface and knead very gently. Place in the tin and cover with foil. Bake for about 50 minutes, then remove the foil and bake for a further 10 minutes until the top is nicely browned. Turn out on to a wire rack to cool. Eat at once.

This is an old Scottish recipe for simple, wholesome bread which requires no proving.

Lemon Tarts

BASE
3 oz. flour   2 oz. butter   ¾ oz. icing sugar   2 teaspoons cold water

FILLING
The juice of a small lemon   2 oz. caster sugar   1 egg   Icing sugar for dusting

Set oven to 375°F or Mark 5. Grease deep patty tins (makes approximately six tarts). Sift the flour into a bowl. Rub in the butter and add the icing sugar. Add sufficient of the water to make a moist dough. Roll out on a floured surface, cut into rounds and line the patty tins. Bake blind for 10 minutes. Remove from the oven and reduce temperature to 350°F or Mark 4. Meanwhile beat together the egg, caster sugar and lemon juice. Fill the pastry cases with the mixture and bake until set and the pastry is nicely browned. Serve hot or cold, but do not chill in the refrigerator.

Marmalade Cake

8 oz. self-raising flour	2 tablespoons orange marmalade
2 eggs, beaten	1 teaspoon finely grated rind
3 oz. caster sugar	of an orange
4 oz. margarine	2 tablespoons milk
1 drop vanilla essence	Pinch of salt

Set oven to 350°F or Mark 4. Grease a 6 inch round cake tin. Sift the flour and salt into a bowl. Rub in the margarine until the mixture resembles fine breadcrumbs. Stir in the sugar and half the orange rind and then add the eggs, marmalade, milk and vanilla essence. Mix well together to the consistency of a thick batter. Transfer to the tin and bake in the centre of the oven for approximately 1 hour 20 minutes until golden in colour or until a skewer inserted into the cake comes out clean. Sprinkle the remaining orange rind over the top. Leave in the tin for a few minutes before turning out on to a wire rack to cool.

Crovie, Moray Firth

Plain Oven Scones

8 oz. self-raising flour   ¼ pint buttermilk, full cream milk
2 oz. butter   or soured milk
1 teaspoon caster sugar   Pinch of salt

Set oven to 450°F or Mark 8. Grease and flour a baking sheet. Sift the dry ingredients into a bowl and rub in the butter. Add sufficient of the milk to make a moist and spongy dough. Turn out on to a floured surface and knead gently. Roll out to ½ inch thickness and cut into rounds with a 2½ inch pastry cutter. Place on the baking sheet. Brush the tops with milk and bake for 8-10 minutes until risen and light golden in colour. Cool on a wire rack. Serve split in half with butter and jam.

For rich scones add 1 beaten egg to the dry ingredients before adding sufficient milk. Brush the tops of the scones with beaten egg rather than with milk.

Butterscotch Ice Cream

2 oz. butter   6 level tablespoons dark soft brown sugar
½ pint warm full cream milk   2 eggs   2½ oz. caster sugar
4 drops vanilla essence   10 fl. oz. fresh whipping cream

Melt the brown sugar and butter together in a pan over a gentle heat. Increase the heat until the mixture bubbles for 1 minute only. Allow to cool slightly. Add the warm milk. Stir continuously over a gentle heat until thoroughly blended. Allow to cool. Beat together the eggs and the caster sugar in a bowl. Pour the mixture from the saucepan on to the beaten eggs/sugar, add the vanilla essence and stir. Strain back into the pan. Stir over a low heat until the mixture thickens slightly; take care not to let it boil. Cool the mixture. Whip the cream lightly and fold into the cooled mixture. Pour into a freezer container and freeze until mushy. Beat with a whisk and return to the freezer until the ice cream is firm.

Almond Shortbread Biscuits

6 oz. flour   **5 oz. butter**
2 oz. cornflour   **1 oz. ground almonds**
3 oz. caster sugar

Set oven to 350°F or Mark 4. Grease a baking sheet. Cream the butter in a mixing bowl. Sift together the flour and cornflour and add, with the almonds and sugar, to the butter. Work the ingredients together with the hands. Turn out on to a very lightly floured surface and finish kneading until the dough is smooth. Roll the dough into two rounds each ¼ inch thick. Prick well with a fork and mark each circle into six triangles. Transfer to the baking sheet. Bake for about 25-30 minutes. Allow to cool slightly before cutting and then place on a wire rack to finish cooling.

Black Cuillins from Elgol

Apple Plate Cake

8 oz. self-raising flour   4 oz. butter   2 oz. caster sugar
4 cooking apples   1 egg, beaten   A little milk
Melted butter for glazing
Ground cloves or cinnamon and caster sugar for dusting

Set oven to 425°F or Mark 7. Grease an 8 inch round flan tin. Rub the butter into the flour in a bowl and stir in the sugar. Peel and grate two of the apples and add to the flour with the beaten egg. Mix well together. If the dough is rather firm add a little milk to soften. Turn the dough on to a floured surface and knead lightly. Press evenly into the base of the tin. Peel, core and slice the remaining apples and arrange, neatly overlapping, on top of the dough. Brush with melted butter and sprinkle with a pinch of ground cloves or cinnamon and a little caster sugar. Bake for 25-30 minutes and serve warm.

Honey and Orange Tea Loaf

6 oz. self raising flour	1 level teaspoon baking powder
6 oz. honey	6 tablespoons milk
1 oz. margarine	Grated rind of 1 large orange
1 egg	Pinch of salt
Clear honey to glaze	

Set oven to 350°F or Mark 4. Grease and line a 2 lb. loaf tin. Cream the margarine and honey together in a bowl, mixing thoroughly. Add the egg and beat vigorously. Sieve the flour, salt and baking powder and add alternately with the milk, to the creamed mixture. Sprinkle in the orange rind and mix well. Spoon the mixture into the tin. Bake for 45 minutes. Remove from the oven, glaze with honey and return to the oven for a further 10 minutes. Remove from the tin and cool on a wire rack. Serve sliced and buttered.

METRIC CONVERSIONS

The weights, measures and oven temperatures used in the preceding recipes can be easily converted to their metric equivalents. The conversions listed below are only approximate, having been rounded up or down as may be appropriate.

Weights

Avoirdupois	Metric
1 oz.	just under 30 grams
4 oz. (¼ lb.)	app. 115 grams
8 oz. (½ lb.)	app. 230 grams
1 lb.	454 grams

Liquid Measures

Imperial	Metric
1 tablespoon (liquid only)	20 millilitres
1 fl. oz.	app. 30 millilitres
1 gill (¼ pt.)	app. 145 millilitres
½ pt.	app. 285 millilitres
1 pt.	app. 570 millilitres
1 qt.	app. 1.140 litres

Oven Temperatures

	°Fahrenheit	Gas Mark	°Celsius
Slow	300	2	150
	325	3	170
Moderate	350	4	180
	375	5	190
	400	6	200
Hot	425	7	220
	450	8	230
	475	9	240

Flour as specified in these recipes refers to plain flour unless otherwise described.